They w

Effortlessly, buckets in tow

They walk without worry

Or water aflow

To them, it comes so easily

Without effort or strain

To them, there is no problem

To keep their water contained

I walk behind, wet Earth underfoot

The water spills out and I feel ashamed

I struggle and stumble, water seeping down the sides

The water pours out and I feel to blame

Until I look down and see the difference

Their buckets are solid, complete and whole

My bucket is unalike, water flows out

My bucket is different, it has holes

Chapter 1
The Early Years

I was four. Her nails were red, her hair was curly. We were in a room that had toys, a bean bag chair, and a small table. She laughed as she pulled me around. My small body sat inside a cardboard box which she dragged around the room. I laughed as she pulled me to a stop.

"Okay," she said. "Time's up."

"Awww," I said.

"I'll see you next time, okay?" She said as she patted my head.

My mom came into the room and we walked into the waiting room. I didn't want to leave. I enjoyed going to see her. I didn't know why I saw her, or why my mom took me to see her, but I saw her a lot. We played with toys and we painted a lot. She was the one person who actively played with me. I enjoyed my time with her, whatever the reason was for it, I enjoyed it.

"Goodbye, Sarah!" The receptionist called as we walked towards the doors.

"Mom, one more piece, please!" I cried.

"Sure, go ahead," she said.

I ran to the counter and reached for the bowl of candy.

"Can I?" I asked.

"Of course," the receptionist said as she pushed the candy bowl towards me. I picked out a red lollipop and said thanks as I ran towards my mom who was waiting at the door for me.

The visits continued. I don't remember how often I saw her, but in my little kid eyes, it was a lot. It felt like every other day. We played with puppets, painted a mask, played with clay and dolls. At some point, I started to take a medication.

"What's this?" I asked my mom one evening as she handed me a pill from a prescription pill bottle.

"Something to help you sleep." She said.

Sleeping was an issue. I hated night time. It was when everyone left me and I was all alone. I would sometimes sit cross legged on my bed in tears. Sometimes, my heart would beat really fast, I would hyperventilate, I felt like screaming but I couldn't. I felt like clawing my skin off. Those were the worst nights. Those were the nights I feared. I would feel my heart start to race when my mom announced it was bedtime because I was afraid I would die. I hated when everyone fell asleep and left me alone.

When I did sleep, I would have horrific vulgar dreams. The dreams about blood, witches, knives and death would wake me in tears. I would fight sleep for the rest of the night for fear of the dreams coming back.

Sometimes, I would sleep with my mom and dad. I would quietly crawl into their bed after they had fallen asleep and I would snake my way in between them where I would sleep soundly. Night after night, I began to sneak into their room to hide from the dreams and to hide from the pounding heart while sitting on my bed. After a while, my mom says around age 7, they started to lock their bedroom door. So I began to sleep in the hallway, with my hand touching their door. The lady that played with me suggested we get a small pet to keep in my bedroom. So we got a hamster. I wasn't exactly sure what the hamster was supposed to do, but it mostly ran on it's wheel while I sat on my bed hyperventilating and crying. If it was supposed to be a comfort animal, it was failing miserably.

One play session with the lady with curly hair she said it was our last time playing together. I didn't know why. I felt like she didn't like me anymore. She took one of my paintings that I had excitedly dumped copious amounts of glitter on, wrote my name and age on the back, along with "I will miss you!, Love Janet". She also gave me a mask I had painted with red and blue. She had told me earlier that the blue was sadness and the red was anger. I didn't understand how she knew that, I just thought the colors were pretty. After that session, I never saw her again. I also stopped taking the nightly medication. I didn't know why.

My family was normal. About as normal as normal can be. My parents were loving and caring. We laughed over family dinners, had pizza night, went to the movies, played at the park, walked to school, had birthday parties and Christmas mornings. The only abnormality was actually abnormally normal. My biological father had left when I was born. The man I called my dad began to date my mom when I was an infant. He was my dad. But in the mid 90's it was pretty normal to have this factor in your family dynamics. Thankfully, unlike other broken families, mine affected me very little. My dad had been there from the very beginning. I had a strong male role model who loved me and guided me despite my biological father's absence. I often forgot, and still forget, that I am not blood related to my dad. In the third grade I filled out a family tree and put all of his information. It wasn't until it was graded and handed back that I realized my simple and undetectable error.

My mother had a bag of old sepia toned photos in her closet. Most of them were from a wedding. Her wedding. A man with dark curly hair and a dark beard stood next to her. Another picture showed him standing next to an 80's car and waving at the camera. Another one showed them posing next to a rock. Most were from the wedding. She told me he had Bipolar Disorder. And a love for cocaine. She told me that he would become violent with rage and then sink to depression. He coped with cocaine. He missed my birth because he was out getting his fix. She left soon after I was born. Or he left. I'm not sure on technicalities of that, but what matters is that he was out of my life forever. Or so I thought.

Around the age of 10, we moved to California where I joined a 5th grade class part way through the school year. I worried about fitting in. They listened to rap music on a walkman at lunch time. I had never heard rap music before, but I liked it. I forgot about my "playdates" with Janet. I worried about who was supposedly kissing who, and who got caught holding hands. A boy named Johnny asked me to play basketball with him one time. I was too nervous to play a game I had never played before, and he seemed embarrassed when I told him no.

One time a group of us were sitting on a picnic table during lunch. Someone brought up virginity. I didn't know what that meant. When it was asked who was a virgin, almost everyone said yes. When they asked me, I said "I don't think so, what's that?" and they laughed. I laughed too.

The sixth grade started and I started to shave my legs. I found out what virginity was. I had a crush on a boy named Oscar, but I was much taller than he was. In fact, I was the tallest girl in class. So I sunk in my chair to make myself appear small and petite like the other girls. We had different classrooms and different teachers throughout the day. This was to prepare us for high school. We also had an agenda with the days of the week listed and our classes listed to keep ourselves organized.

In this agenda, I started to draw arrows. Simple arrows, up and down. Up was what I loved. I felt full of energy, productive, social, happy, confident. I would volunteer for extra work, start new projects, sign up for clubs and do exceptionally well on tests because of all of my hours of hyper-focussed studying I had done the night before in lieu of sleep. I loved the up arrows.

The down arrows were awful. I would draw sad faces in my agenda too. I would write poetry about self mutilation. I would fantasize about self mutilation. When riding in our family car I would think about unbuckling my seat belt, opening the car door, and jumping out while we drove down the freeway. I hated school on these days. I hated the teachers. I felt emptiness. Numb. I was incapable of experiencing joy. It is like when you get a sinus infection and you are unable to smell and taste food. Except my sinus infection was a brain infection and I was unable to experience joy and contentment. I hated my down arrow days. On these days, I would try to go to the nurse's office for a "stomach ache" so I could be sent home. After about the tenth time, my mom instructed the nurse to ignore my complaints and send me back to class.

I noticed a pattern. I would have weeks of down arrow days followed by 2-3 up arrow days. Once, on an up arrow day, we went shopping and we bought new clothes. I wore my new clothes to school the next day and felt glorious in my new outfit. The next day, and weeks, were down arrows. So the next time we went shopping, I wore one new article of clothing to school a day for a week, hoping that by spacing out all the new clothes I would put off the down arrow days, or maybe even prevent them. It didn't work. The up arrow days continued. The down arrow days overstayed their welcome. Up and down, up and down.

When I was 11, I worked in the library as an elective. One day I had grown so restless with death and dying, my own in fact, that I hid in a book closet. I didn't understand what I was feeling or what was going on. So I hid and I cried because I wanted this day to end, forever. I couldn't work at the library counter, so I hid.

The door opened, and my peer, Kristan, walked in.

"What are you doing?" She asked.

"I don't know. I'm having a bad day." I said. A down arrow day.

She knelt down. "What's going on?"

"I feel like killing myself," I whispered. I expected her to laugh at me.

"Come on," She said. "We're going to the school counselor. That's where I went when I felt that way last year. You need to talk to her."

I followed her as she whispered something to the librarian, and we walked towards a room across the quad area.

The door opened and a lady I had never seen before said hello. Kristan waved and told me good luck. I sat down in an empty chair. The lady sat down.

"Hello, I am Bonnie, the school psychologist. What brings you here today?"

I looked around the room. I whispered. "I want to kill myself."

"Oh. And why's that?" She asked as if there would be a specific reason.

"I don't know.." I said.

"Have you felt this way for a while?" She asked

"A few weeks I think" I said. But I didn't tell her I had actually felt that way off and on all the time. It was normal, to me, to feel this way. It was my normal.

She asked basic depression questions, the same questions they ask when screening for depression. How are you sleeping? Eating? Are you unable to enjoy things you usually do? Etc. and so on.

"We need to get you to the Mental Health Department right away." She said.

To my surprise, I was escorted to the office where she spoke with the attendance liaison who then called my mother to come pick me up.

My mom arrived. "Really, Sarah?" she said. "I had to leave work and use my vacation hours."

I felt really guilty for causing all the commotion. And I became angry with Kristan for taking me to the counselor. She should have just let me cry alone in the closet by myself.

We drove in silence to the Mental Health Department. My mom and I arrived at the reception area where she explained what the school had told her. I didn't listen. I just watched the tv mounted in the corner. A little while later my name was called.

I followed a woman down a hallway full of doorways until we reached an open door. Inside was a white table with two chairs. She sat down in one, and I sat in the other. I noticed that her blue eye eyeliner was uneven.

"Hello, Sarah." She said. "How are you?"

"Ok, I guess." I said.

"Alright," she said. "I got a phone call from your school that you seem to be experiencing depression and are having suicidal thoughts? Is that correct?"

"Yeah, I guess so." I said.

"Ok, well, let me have you fill out this questionnaire and I will be right back," she said as she handed me a sheet of paper and a pencil.

She left the room and I looked down at the paper. The same questions they always ask. How are you sleeping? How are you eating? Are you unable to enjoy activities that you typically enjoy? Do you feel numb or excessive sadness? Has this been continuous for a period of at least two weeks?

Check. Check. Yes. Double check. Checkity check check check.

"Wow", she said when she was finished reviewing my paper. "It seems like you are experiencing an episode of major depression." She put the paper down.

"Is there anything unusual going on? A death in the family? Divorce? Anything like that?" she asked.

"No, everything is normal." I said. In fact, having depression was normal for me.

"Okay", she said. "I am going to start you on a low dose of Paxil, make sure you get this to the pharmacy right away and start taking it today, ok?" she asked.

We left the Mental Health Department. I handed the prescription slip to my mom who promised to fill it as she dropped me back off at school for the rest of the day.

I started to take the Paxil. I didn't notice anything for the first few weeks. My arrows still went up and down. But after a few weeks, I noticed my down arrow days went more down. I became more depressed. I was more suicidal than ever before. Over a period of months I became more and more depressed. I continued to see the lady with the blue eyeliner a few times but I don't remember ever telling her anything of substance, or her telling me anything of substance.

What I do remember however, is the last day that I saw her.

We walked into the room with the white table. My mom came with me this time. It was an up arrow day.

"How are you doing?" She asked.

"Great!" I said excitedly. I told her about a high test score I had received and that I had joined the multicultural club at school and I had spent the day before playing soccer at lunch and I had spent the evening studying for a geography test. I didn't tell her that I hadn't really slept in a few days and that I felt like jumping out of my skin. My energetic enthusiasm was mistaken for an end to depression.

"Well," she said. "It looks like your depression has ended. I see no need to continue you on the Paxil or continue seeing you. But if you ever feel that way again, please make sure to let your mom know so you can come back here, okay?"

"Great! Okay! Thank you so much!" I said with a huge grin. I had been cured! Finally! After all these years of torment I was all better, hooray!

My mom and I left, and we were both glad that we were done with the appointments and medication. The medication made me feel worse anyway.

A week later the down arrows came back, and I cried. I cried because I thought they were gone forever, like the lady with the blue eyeliner had said. I cried because I was tired of the down arrow days. I thought I was cured.

I didn't tell my parents. I didn't tell anyone this time. I didn't want anyone to have to take time off of work. I didn't want to see the lady with the blue eyeliner again and tell her "Oops, sorry, just kidding!" so I kept it to myself. I fantasized about taking a knife and cutting my arms. I fantasized about holding myself under the bathtub water until I stopped breathing. I stopped going to the multicultural club. I got poor grades on the tests that week. I wished I could fall asleep forever.

The arrows continued to go up and down, though they were mostly down. I began to hate school. My whole body would ache. My arms would feel heavy. All I wanted to do was sleep for a thousand years. I didn't want to eat. I just wanted to sleep forever.

My poetry book became filled with suicidal themed poems. Self mutilation poetry also spilled onto the pages. I began to go on the internet and print out pictures of how I felt. One picture in particular comes to mind. It was of a boy, who leaned over his bathroom counter and appeared to be screaming. In the bathroom mirror was an imagine of himself who instead of screaming, was calmly holding a gun to his head. I related to the picture so I printed it out and glued it to my poetry book.

My parents liked that I was writing poetry. They told me that I was destined to be a writer. No one was allowed to read my book though, and I made sure of it because it was always in my possession. In those pages were my darkest thoughts. My hopes and dreams were nowhere to be found, but my fantasies about killing myself were there for no one to read. My days continued to be more down, for weeks, for months.

I printed out more disturbing images and poems from the internet. I created a binder to hold all of them. They were about guns, death, and anger. One evening, my mom found the binder. I came home from school and she was holding it.

"We need to talk," she said.

"Okay?" I said sarcastically. I was 13 now. Sarcasm was my language.

"What is this?" she asked. "Are you okay? Should I be worried?"

"What?" I asked, and then saw the binder.

I rolled my eyes. "No mom, It's just stuff. It doesn't mean anything."

"Are you sure," she asked.

"Yeah mom, totally sure." I said as I rolled my eyes and reached for the binder.

The up and down continued, as it always has.

A few years later, I was sitting in my room when it hit me. I was experiencing an "episode of major depression", as the lady with the blue eyeliner put it. I needed to go back to the room with the white table. I realized that I had never been cured at all. I realized that my depression was just getting worse and I needed help.

I opened my bedroom door. My mom happened to be standing on the other side. "Mom?" I asked. I had tears streaming down my face.

"What?" she asked.

"I think I'm depressed again. I feel suicidal again." I said. Please take me, I silently begged.

"Oh honey, it's just your teenage hormones. You're fine." She said confidently.

I closed the door.

My anxiety was continuous throughout my childhood. What began as panic attacks on my bed at night grew into me being panicky about nearly every aspect of my life. I was labeled a "worry wart" and it was embarrassing. I worried about everything and anything. I began picking at my cuticles until they bled when I was young. I sometimes wore bandages to hide my self inflicted wounds. I would hyperventilate and pace the floor for hours.

In high school my up arrow days grew into being hyper productive on things other than school work. I once began to paint a mural on my bedroom wall. I skipped school for three days to paint. I painted for hours. When it became dark I turned on lamps so I could continue painting.

Several times, I would come up with some grand idea of a website. I would spend 2-4 days obsessively programming, only leaving the computer chair to pee. Sweat would pour down from my armpits and I would feverishly type away at whatever it was that I was doing. Numerous times, I would come up with an amazing idea for a book, and I would spend 2-4 days writing this book, disregarding personal hygeine, school work (and school altogether), social relationships and other responsibilities. I would stay awake until 5 am, then turn off the lights, turn off the computer and crawl into bed to pretend like I was sleeping so when my parents came in to wake me up at 6am, I would yawn well rested and go about my day. The paint would be put away, the computer turned off. On some of these up arrow days, I would drive to school, sit through first period, and then leave through the side gate just before second period. In the attendance guidelines, it stated that a truancy was defined as missing ALL class periods for the day, so I made sure to attend at least one class most days. Luckily, I still graduated with a decent grade average and 67 "truancies". They have since redefined what a truancy actually is. The majority of those truancies were actually truancies where I skipped school to go to the mall with friends or was self medicating by drinking at a party house. But a portion of those truancies were from my up-arrow days where I became so obsessed with a project that I would spend 2-4 days, sometimes longer, obsessively pouring my heart and soul into this project.

And then, it would slam to a stop. My obsession and passion would come grinding to a halt. After a few days of programming, writing, painting or researching, I would all of a sudden stop. STOP. Out of nowhere, someone would pull a drain and every last drop of passion, productivity, excitement, will to live, happiness and light would swirl around a drain and leave me there, empty. Holding a paintbrush standing in my bedroom. Sitting in front of a computer and staring at 43 pages of a typed novel. Staring at a half-built website. STOP.

I have always felt like my life had a certain purpose. I always thought that I was destined to be something spectacular. My up arrow days, I am certain that I will be the next Hemingway, or Van Gogh, or whatever. I am certain that I am meant to be working on this special spectacular project that this special spectacular time. I feel like this is my "moment", this is what I have been waiting for. And then the drain is pulled, and down I go. I fall for this trick over and over and over in high school. Over and over I go up and down.

At 16, I decided I was broken. Depression is supposed to be years long, caused by a death or divorce. Then it goes away for good, never to be seen again. I was broken. My depression comes and goes like the tide of the ocean. My mood goes up and down like the waves of the ocean which are dictated to do so by the moon. I was still unaware of the meaning of my up arrow days, but I had decided that I was just broken. I had gone back to the mental health department then. It was the same as the time before. They asked me the list of depression symptoms which I had memorized not because I had read them but because I had lived them. I was prescribed an antidepressant that made me feel more depressed. So I stopped taking it, and I was broken.

I was 18, I decided I would overcome my depression on my own. This would be partially from ignoring it and just continuing on with my life, and partially from pretending I had never had a problem in the first place. It was just hormones. I was just seeking attention, wasn't I? It was all just teenage angst. I drank and partied at every opportunity. I never tried street drugs. I know my biological father was an addict, so I refused to even try them. I refused to end up like him.

Chapter 2
The forgotten years

I was 25. I was sitting in my desk at the community college in classroom 220. The teacher was male, about my age. He was teaching science. But I knew. I knew that he had a crush on me. I sat in the front of the class that day. As he passed out our next assignment, I waited for him to come by my desk. As he walked by I waited for his eye contact or a slight gesture. He smiled. I knew it! He was in love with me. I tapped my foot incessantly, my knee bouncing up and down as it had been for over an hour. The inside of my body felt like it was full of tiny metallic balls that were vibrating. Oh, how I wish we could have class outside. My knee continued to bounce up and down, up and down. The teacher was talking about something, I'm not sure. I couldn't follow along. I tried to, but I couldn't. I felt like screaming. Just letting out the kept in energy. I felt like my toes and fingers were shooting off laser beams of energy. I couldn't take it anymore. I gathered my things and left. I hoped that the teacher wouldn't be too upset, I knew that he still wanted to sleep with me so maybe he would let it slide. I walked out the door and headed towards my car. Everyone was looking at me. They all wanted to sleep with me. I had a big yellow flower in my hair that matched my yellow skirt. I wore yellow eye shadow and red lipstick. I was a sex goddess and everyone wanted a piece.

When I got home, I saw my neighbor checking his mail. So I waved. I waved excessively and excitedly. I didn't even know his name, I had never waved to him before. I felt an urge to walk across the street and tell him about my class and the teacher and my big idea. I refrained and went inside. I decided that it would be a good idea to clean the house. So I began to clean the living room with unwavering energy and motivation. Every surface was swept or mopped or bleached or dusted. Hours had passed. I was in the closet organizing my clothes when I started to feel a drip from my nose. Blood began to drop onto my arm drip by drop. I wiped it away and carried on with reorganizing the closet from the floor to the ceiling. I found a dirty sock and held it to my nose for a few minutes. I didn't have the patience to stop moving so I held the sock with one hand and continued to moved things around with another.

By the time I had come out of the closet, night had fallen. I was trembling. I felt like I had drank several pots of coffee when I had not drank any. I felt like jumping up and down and doing jumping jacks. I felt like bouncing on the bed.

I couldn't sleep. I tried to sleep but my mind kept moving and my bouncing knee now felt like my bouncing body. I decided to get up and work on an assignment. I pulled out the computer, put music on my headphones and went to work. By 5am, I had written 18 pages. I began to browse the internet. As I was browsing I came up with a brilliant beyond brilliant idea. It needed a website though. So I set to work.

I installed the needed programs and began to build the website, obsessing over perfection of every line and every letter. Hours passed. Before I knew it, it was the evening. I had skipped a day of classes. I continued to build the website, only stopping to go to the bathroom. I just knew this idea was what I was born for. I would win awards for it. This was my destiny. I was brilliant. Pecking away at the keyboard my body still felt like it was vibrating. I wanted to clean again but the house was already clean. So I obsessed over lines and colors and fonts and letters. Hours and hours passed. It was the next day. I decided this idea was far too important to stop pursuing. School would have to wait. With this idea, I wouldn't need school anyways, so who cares. I could just stop altogether. If anyone tried to call my phone I either ignored them or answered impatiently and got off the phone as soon as possible. I was busy pursuing my destiny. My brilliance had no time to waste.

Then, sometime around 3pm, after three days had passed, I stopped. STOP.

I stared at the computer screen and saw that my idea was worthless. I highlighted everything I had done and hit "delete". I turned off the computer. What a waste. I wasted two days of class on nothing. I was nothing. This was nothing.

I grew tired. So very tired. What a loser. What a pathetic waste of space I was. My arms grew heavy. My body felt like it weighed a thousand pounds. I went to bed.

When I woke up the next morning I cried. I cried and cried. I couldn't get out of bed. My body was too achey, too heavy. I cried because I couldn't go to class. I was going to have to drop my classes, again. I felt guilty for leaving my class the other day. I felt guilty for not attending my classes. I felt guilty for being alive. I felt guilty for feeling guilty. I felt ashamed for being such a loser. Such a waste of space. I had no right to be alive. I began to fantasize about ways to kill myself.

Dear (Professor),

I am terribly sorry but I have come down with (horrible illness) and was unable to attend classes this week. I have gone to the doctor and got medication so I imagine that I will be able to attend classes beginning Monday or shortly thereafter.

Sincerely,
Sarah

I had an overwhelming urge to stab my right thigh. There is a distinct frustration and feeling when you are driving down the street and the bottom of your foot itches. You need to keep your hands on the steering wheel and stay focused on the road but so badly you want to tear off your shoe and claw at the bottom of your foot.

That same frustration and urge is present when I felt like I wanted to stab my thigh. I hyperventilated and cried. I thought of ways I could kill myself and spare my family and friends of having to deal with me. Weed killer, gun, pain pills, a rope, slitting my wrists and sitting in the bathtub so I didn't make a mess. The mess was the issue because no matter what I did, there would be a mess; there would be a body. I wanted to just disappear. I wanted to just float away. I wanted to painlessly never wake up, and I wanted my family to never shed a tear over me. I wanted to just cease to exist and never have existed in the first place. I wanted so badly to just stop everything. I wanted to stop breathing. I wanted to stop feeling. I wanted to just stop.

I dropped my classes, as I had done before. Today at 30 years old I have attempted to restart college a total of 6 different times. It always ended the same way. I have been enrolled at the same college for 10 years yet I don't even have a 2-year degree.

My down days debilitated me. I was unable to function as an adult. I became lifeless. I craved to be lifeless. I couldn't shower. I couldn't drive. I couldn't hold conversations. I had obsessive continuous thoughts of hurting myself and killing myself. I saw little brown furry animals scurrying across the floor. I saw the furniture breathing.

My up days debilitated me too sometimes. Sometimes they are hyper productive and I was able to focus. Those around me were clueless to what was going on. I just seemed excessively happy, social, funny, energetic and productive. I just seemed to be having a really good day for a few days in a row. But sometimes this energy is put towards something ridiculous, like a website or painting a collage that I never finished.

Never finishing my projects is the biggest downside. While I may have a brilliant idea or a lame idea, it always ends the same way, which is stopping before it is complete. My endless ideas and projects and books and paintings are always incomplete. It is so shameful to have never followed through with any of my hypomanic projects. I am crossing my fingers that I finish this book and see it through to the end because it will be my first time ever completing a project.

But sometimes my up days are excessively anxious and irritable. I want to rip the clicking ceiling fan out of the ceiling. I go on my porch and take all the windchimes down and shove them in a box. The leafblower down the street makes me want to scream. I pound my fist on the table and yell in anger. Nothing is moving fast enough for me. I become impatient at a stoplight and someone cuts me off, so I run them off the road into the dirt. No one is driving fast enough for me. Everyone needs to get out of my way. I pace the floor with worry over everything my mind can come up with. I worry about the present, the past and the future. I pace and pace until my legs ache but I don't stop. I pace and rub my head repeatedly over and over with worry. Pieces of hair begin to break off in my hand as I rub my head continuously. My heart feels like it is going to explode. I try to sleep but my mind won't stop moving. It circles over and over rehashing what it just told me. It doesn't stop, so I don't stop. I pace the floor as my mind swirls faster and faster.

I begin to have a panic attack. My heart beats rapidly and I begin to breathe faster and faster. It feels like I am breathing through a straw. I drop to my knees and I can't move. I grab my chest, certain I am having a heart attack. I can't talk. I can't move. I can barely breathe. It feels like I am floating above my body. My brain tells me to calm down but my body won't listen. It ends in ten minutes and I cry.

Finally I calm down after days of pacing the floor and not sleeping. My anxiety never goes away, but it stops being so controlling. I can finally sleep. I can finally tolerate noises and being patient. I can finally breathe. But the depression takes hold again and I wrap in blankets like a sad burrito. I lay in bed for hours or even days. The thoughts of killing myself come back and I decide to follow through this time. I know I am a burden to my family, to the world. I know it is because I love my family that I have to do it. I can't allow my weirdness to rule my life anymore. My quirks control my days and I am tired of it. My family deserves better. I am a lemon and they should be free of my sour life. What a waste of space. What a waste of life.

Chapter 3
The Revelation

I was 29. I sat on the kitchen floor.

Four days ago, I had an idea. I was going to run a business. I researched for hours. I hadn't slept in four days. I applied for loans to finance my business. I decided on a name. I began writing a business proposal. My business idea was revolutionary. I was going to change the world. My idea was genius. I didn't sleep. I barely ate. I paced the floor and told my husband over and over and over about my ideas, repeating the same sentences and jumbling together my words. I had to keep talking. I had to keep telling him. I hopped up and down on the porch and grinned from ear to ear. I was going to be famous. My idea was incredible. I was unstoppable. I skipped three days of work. I skipped three days of classes. It didn't matter. I was going to be famous. I didn't need that job. My degree was pointless.

And then suddenly, after hours of research and writing and obsessing, it stopped.

Just like that.

I blinked, and every ounce of creativity, desire, excitement and determination, had left.

In rolled the fog of depression. My familiar foe that had haunted me since I could remember. By mid-afternoon, I was sitting on the kitchen floor counting the minutes until my husband came home from work. I wanted to kill myself. I couldn't think of a way to painlessly do it. Knives sounded like a good idea, but isn't that usually not final? We didn't have any pills except regular cabinet medications. There was nowhere in the house strong enough to support my hanging body.

So I sat on the kitchen floor and waited.

He came home and I told him. As we sat on the porch, he browsed his phone.

"Honey, I think you are bipolar." He said as he handed me his phone.

"What? No I'm not." I rolled my eyes.

"No, read this. This is you." And he shoved the phone in my face.

Bipolar Type II. The article listed symptoms. I read them. And I read them again. And again.

My heart thumped. I began to sweat. I clicked on another link, and another. I read articles and lists of symptoms and personal accounts. In detective novels, there is a moment where the lead detective discovers a key piece of evidence that suddenly solves the crime. In that moment, he gasps and says "Oh my god" as he realizes the truth.

"Oh my god", I gasped, like a detective. "That's me! This is me!" I began to cry. And I read more articles and links with each one I saw myself more and more. The depression. The obsessions. The "intermittent ADHD", the obsessive cleaning, the writing, the delusions, the sleepless nights, the days that I couldn't get out of bed.

The more I read, the more I realized that this has been me all along. My whole life. My phobia to vomit, my severe anxiety, all of it was connected and intertwined.

"What do I do?" I asked. I had been researching all day. It was dark.

"I don't know. Go see a doctor I guess." He hugged me.

It took some work but I was able to see a therapist four days later.

"Have you been feeling excessively sad, every day, all day, for longer than a two week period?" She asked. The lights were dim. She yawned. Her computer screen was turned away from me. She didn't make eye contact.

"Yes." I said. With each question, I lost faith. I had waited four days for this assessment.

"Have you lost interest in activities, lost desire to complete school, work or household duties?" She yawned and stared at her computer screen.

"Yes, but sometimes I become obsessive." I said. I had to save this appointment. I had to do something.

She looked at me and raised her eyebrow. "Four more questions", she said, and clicked her mouse.

The questions continued. I knew them by heart. Yes, because I had gone through this same depression questionnaire countless times with other therapists, but also because I knew them by heart. The list of symptoms was memorized because my heart felt these symptoms over and over again.

"That's it." She said as she clicked her mouse. "You seem to be experiencing some depression. I will schedule you with a doctor to begin medication."

That can't be it. There has to be more.

"That's it?", I asked. "There aren't more questions?"

Her computer powered down and she stood up, gathering her jacket and purse. It had been an hour. She yawned.

"What do you mean?" She said as she began to open the office door.

"There should be more questions. Sometimes there are other things. Sometimes I am so hyper I can't sleep. I think I might be bipolar."

She raised her eyebrows and sat her purse on the chair.

"Do you abuse drugs?"

"Well, no..."

"Have you ever been arrested?"

"No, of course not."

"Have you ever done anything dangerous or spontaneous?" She asked, picking up her purse again.

"Well, once I drove to the ocean in the middle of the night."

She opened the office door and said "That's not that unusual. Bipolar is very obvious. You've never been arrested. You aren't a drug user." She headed down the hallway. "Let's get you set up with a doctor so you can begin a medication regimen."

Two months later, I sat in the waiting room. A woman next to me rocked and moaned in her chair. Every few rocks she would whimper. I wondered what the doctor would look like. My stomach was in knots. I had waited two months to see him. This time, they would listen to me. Whoever this doctor is, they would listen to me. I made sure they would listen, I would force them to. I had spent an hour the day before listing out my symptoms. It was two pages long. I included my history, the anxiety at age 4, the depression at age 11. The business ideas, the noises I heard that weren't there, the hypersexuality, the delusions, the sleepless nights. I had the stapled papers folded neatly in my purse. I would make the doctor read the list. I would make him listen.

"Sarah?" An old man poked his head through the door. I smiled and followed him. He left behind a trail of cigarette smoke smell as we walked down the hallway.

"Sorry to keep you waiting, I am a very busy person." He said as he entered his office.

I sat down in the chair across from his desk. "It's fine," I smiled.

"Well, what are we here for, depression?"

I swallowed. "Well, yes and no."

"What do you mean?" He asked with his eyebrows raised.

"Well, I really don't believe that I just have depression. The woman I saw before you did an assessment for depression, which I have, which I have ALWAYS had, but I think there is something else going on."

He sighed and logged in to his computer. After a few moments he said "Well here it shows your diagnosis as Major Depressive Disorder."

"I know", I said. "But I really don't believe that's accurate. I started having anxiety when I was four and sometimes I don't sleep and..." I stopped. I pulled out my list. "Will you please read this?" I handed over the list. I was shaking.

He sighed, leaned back in his chair and folded his arms. "You're really overestimating my reading capabilities" he said as he leaned forward and snatched the paper.

His eyes scanned the pages. He flipped the first page and quickly moved on to the next.

"Do you have a criminal record?"

"No." I said.

"Do you abuse drugs?"

"No. Well, I do smoke marijuana."

"How often?" He asked as he handed the papers back to me.

"Once a day."

He scooted his chair back towards the desk and folded his hands. "Well, this could all be attributed to drug use. Do your relatives have mental health problems?"

"Drug use? I just started smoking three years ago. I've been this way my whole life." I sighed. "My biological father left when I was an infant. But my mom said he had severe bipolar, as did his brother and father."

"Any hospital visits, what medication was he taking?"

I was growing frustrated. He wasn't listening to me. I wasn't being listened to again. "I have no idea. Again, he left when I was an infant. He is a stranger and I know nothing about him."

He leaned back in his chair and put his hands behind his head. "Listen," he said, "Your symptoms could be due to drug use. I have patients come in all the time that complain about hallucinations but pop positive for amphetamines. You have no criminal record. Your history is irrelevant because I don't have any documentation to prove it. Your mother believing your father had bipolar is irrelevant because you can't tell me what medications he was taking. I don't know what you expected when you came in here. I am not a magician. I can't prescribe some magic pill to make you happy with your life."

I was shocked. "How is all that irrelevant?" I stammered. "I'm not asking for a magic pill. I am happy with my life. I am very happy with my life."

"Have you ever been hospitalized for a manic episode?" He said.

"Well, I"

"Yes, or no", he interrupted my explanation.

"No", I said as I slumped in my chair.

His brow furrowed. I could tell he was getting angry. "I think you have a personality problem. And you are emotionally immature. There aren't pills to fix that. What I can give you is the lowest dose of an anti-depressant and then I will see you in three months. Please close the door on your way out."

The original therapist I had seen had left the company so I called the office and asked about being reassigned to another therapist. After a few weeks, I received a phone call.

"Hello, may I speak to Sarah?"

"This is her," I said into the phone.

"Hi Sarah. My name is Allison. I am a clinician for the dual-diagnostics program. I was hoping to schedule an appointment with you."

"Dual-what? What's that?"

"Dual-Diagnostics. It is a program for people that have mental health problems and struggle with drug use."

"But I don't do drugs. Unless you count coffee, now THAT I am addicted to."

She laughed, "Okay, let me pull up your file. You were referred to me."

After a few moments she said, "It shows here that you have Major Depressive Disorder and Cannabis Dependency?"

"What? Dependency? I do smoke marijuana but I'm not addicted."

"Okay, how often?" She said.

"Once a day, maybe. Depends." I said.

"Alright, I wonder why they listed you as dependent then." She said. "So you are experiencing depression?"

"Well, yes, But that's not all. It's so much more complicated than that." I said.

"What do you mean? What else is going on?", she asked.

And I told her. I listed out the symptoms of Bipolar Type II not because they were listed, but because they were what I experienced. She asked me questions, she asked for examples. We scheduled an appointment for the next day. I didn't have to wait anymore.

"Hello", she said. Her smile was infectious. She reminded me of honey and rainbows. She seemed like the type of person that liked to give a lot of hugs.

I sat down in the chair in her office. On the walls were encouraging quotes, pictures of mountains. She had a bookshelf full of books that were titled with psychology related words. She smiled.

"So where were we?", she said.

"Well, on the phone we were talking about my symptoms. I know I have depression. I really don't want to talk about depression. I am tired of talking about depression. I know the symptoms by heart because I have all of them. But I really feel like I have something else going on."

She listened to me. I told her about my "intermittent adhd", the delusions. the noises, the obsessions, the outbursts, the anxiety, the panic attacks. And she listened.

We spent the next few days, over the course of three appointments, discussing my symptoms in depth. She pulled books out of her bookshelf and read passages to me to see if I could relate to the descriptions. She quizzed me about symptoms for disorders I had never heard of, which I didn't relate to at all. I didn't count my steps. I didn't hear voices. I didn't challenge authority. Each symptom we discussed would circle back around to one disorder: Bipolar Type II.

"So, it appears that you are suffering from Bipolar Type II and you have been for a very long time." She said. "You have every symptom, more than required for diagnosis. So I am going to update your diagnosis, okay?" She smiled.

She pointed to the computer screen. "There, see?" Listed below my name was "Bipolar Type II/Generalized Anxiety Disorder". I smiled. "I wanted to tell you something, but I don't want you to take this the wrong way. Let me think of how to put this without offending you." She said as she sat in her chair quietly.

"Ok," she said. "So I think the problem is you come off as much much higher functioning than you are. You are pleasant, friendly, very well spoken, educated and you appear to be very well adjusted. You are much lower functioning than you appear and it only becomes apparent after talking to you for a while. I think that's why you have had such a hard time getting people to listen to you because you appear to be just fine." She paused.

"I think this is from suffering for so long and your desire to hide your symptoms. You were not raised in a mentally supportive time period so you trained yourself to hide your symptoms and pretend to be normal. I think this is why you have had a hard time getting help. Of course, this

does not excuse the doctor's behavior with you, but it might explain why people have not listened to you. You appear to be fine, but you are not." She smiled. "I think it would be a good idea to set up another appointment with the doctor with this new diagnosis to be sure you are receiving the correct medication. Also, let's get you set up with weekly therapy appointments with me. What is a good day for you?"

After the appointment, I went to the receptionist to reschedule another appointment with the doctor. Maybe he would listen to me this time.

My appointment was at ten. It was 10:45 and I had not been called in yet. Finally, the old man poked his head through the door.

"Sarah?" he asked. I followed him down the hall. "I am a very important person here, hence the delay", he said.

We arrived to his office. He didn't sit down. Neither did I.

"Why are you here? I saw you three weeks ago. Is there a problem?"

I was shaking. I was terrified.

"Well", I said. "I have been thoroughly assessed by a therapist and she and I believe that I have Bipolar Type II. Her recommendation was to follow-up with you to ensure that my prescribed medication would work with this more accurate diagnosis."

"Who is this that you saw?"

"Allison Lastname", I said.

"Well, I am much more qualified than her. As you can see from the degrees on my wall, I am an expert and she is not at all. I have already prescribed your medication, it has only been three weeks. I am an experienced professional and I do not agree with that diagnosis at all. I suggest you leave my office and find another doctor that will be willing to work with you because I am not willing to work with you."

I didn't say anything. I was trembling.

"Leave my office."

I held back my tears until the waiting room where I filled out a request to change doctors. I began to see a new doctor who accepted my diagnosis and began to start me on a medication regimen. He listened to my complaints, wanted my opinion and was very unlike the other doctor I had seen before.

I began to see Allison weekly. This was the first time since the lady with the cardboard box that I could remember someone actually interacting with me. Everyone else that I had talked to up until this point would beam with pride as they would say "You have depression!", like this was some new found information. I knew I had depression because I was depression. I had the symptoms memorized because I had experienced them for years. I knew the deepest holes of depression. The previous psychiatrists that I saw in my teens and a couple in my 20's would give me three months supply of an antidepressant and then send me on my way. Zoloft. Wellbutrin. Paxil. Cymbalta. And so many others. My depression would grow more severe that I would throw the rest of the three month supply away and I would not go back to the psychiatrist for fear that they would make me take the pills.

But Allison listened. She listened to my complaints of anxiety. I told her about my panic attacks when I was a child. I told her about my worsening phobia to vomit (which does not bode well with motherhood). She listened to me. And she taught me things that I never knew. She told me that I tend to think in catastrophic terms while depressed. I think the worst will happen in a situation. My anxiety takes over and I just know that we will be in a car accident. She also taught me to accept the people that are in my life for who they are, at no fault to them because that is simply who they are. She taught me to forgive.

As I continued to see Allison, I still experienced my up and down days. But now, for the first time since the 6th grade, I was keeping track. I was moving fast. Up and down within a matter of a week. I would go from Mozart to a sad burrito in a matter of days.

One time, about a week after being diagnosed, I was laying in bed on my stomach watching the clock. It was late. The kids were sound asleep. My husband was snoring next to me. I was alone. And then, like a light switch, I felt it. It felt like butterflies entering my toes. I had to write. I had to jump. I had to get up. I slowly got out of bed and quietly closed the door. I turned the light on in the living room, and I paced. I paced the floor back and forth, back and forth. I felt like pulling out my computer and writing a book, another book that I would pour my heart and soul into to then delete after a few days of obsessing. I felt like running. I felt like organizing the kitchen cabinets or mopping the floor or cleaning out the shed.
I put my hands on my head and I cried. For the first time since being diagnosed, I realized what was going on. I was entering a hypomanic episode. I was sick. I have a mental illness and I am sick.I cried because the butterflies wouldn't stop moving. I cried because I used to laugh about my "intermittent ADHD", and now I cry about my hypomania. I paced the floor until morning. I refused to start any projects. I refused to clean. I refused to let the bipolar dictate me, so I paced until my legs were tired.
The next day I tried to sleep. My husband was frustrated that I didn't wake him up so he could be there for me, and I promised that next time I would. I layed in bed in the early afternoon and I tossed and turned for hours. I gave up and rejoined the family in the living room. My hyper activity continued as I began to clean the house and make dinner despite two days with no sleep. Once it became evening

time, I grew scared knowing that my family would fall asleep and leave me alone. I couldn't sleep again, of course. So I spent several hours writing in a makeshift journal on the computer. I finally crashed the following morning when I slept the day away and the evening as well. Along with my energy, my mood crashed too.

The feelings of wanting to kill myself reappeared. I decided my family and children were stuck with this lemon mother that has all these broken pieces. They deserved so much more, so much better. I hid a knife in a bathroom closet. I weeped for seemingly no reason but my reasons were simply; I hated myself. I was a burden. I was a frustration. I was an unwanted parasite. I deserved to be dead. I deserved to be hurt.

Once the family was situated and occupied, I went into the bathroom and locked the door. I pulled my pants down and took the knife I had hid. I began to slice my leg, but he blade was too dull. No matter how hard I pushed, only white lines appeared. I cried because I couldn't even cut myself properly.

"Are you okay?" my husband called.

"Yeah, I'm fine, be out in a sec." I called.

But I wasn't fine. If there had been a shotgun on the floor in that moment, I would have shoved the barrel in my mouth. But we had no guns. Our home was childproof. It was Sarahproof. We owned nothing that could kill, and apparently a knife that can't cut.

The next day the depression grew worse. The kids were at school so I laid in bed and sobbed. My husband tried to console me but there were no words he could say that would make me feel better. He was growing frustrated as was I.

I got up and walked into the bathroom, remembering the knife. As I entered the bathroom I remembered it was too dull, and I couldn't cut myself. I dropped to my knees and sobbed.

"What's wrong, what's wrong?" my husband desperately asked.

"I can't do this anymore", I said to the tile floor.

"Do what? Do you want me to leave?" he asked, confused.

"No. Stay", I sobbed.

I rested my head on the tile floor and then an urge came. So I picked my head up and slammed my forehead into the tile. I banged my head on the tile again and again. I screamed, "I can't do this anymore!!" My husband grabbed me off the floor, carried me to bed and laid next to me.

"You can't hurt yourself," he said.

"Why not?" I asked.

"Because you just can't, Sarah. Stop," he said.

"I can't stop. I have to. I don't want to be alive anymore. I can't do this anymore." I whispered.

"If I leave this room, are you going to try to hurt yourself?" He asked. I let silence pass.

"Yes," I whispered.

"Then I can't leave you alone." he said.

I remembered my prescribed medication was on the fridge, a whole month's supply. I didn't know what would happen if I swallowed the whole bottle but I was determined to find out.

I stood up and headed towards the kitchen through the bathroom. I grabbed the pills off the top of the fridge and shoved them into my pocket.

"Give me the pills, Sarah." He said from behind me.

I reluctantly handed them over and went back to the bedroom. I began to dig through my jewelry box that held a pocket knife. He grabbed me from behind and laid me on the bed. He quickly held my hands down and threw his body weight on me. He used his legs to wrap around my legs. I couldn't get out no matter how much I struggled, no matter how much I wiggled.

"I will hold you for as long as it takes," he said with tears forming in his eyes. "I love you and I will hold you to keep you from hurting yourself. You are my wife and I will protect you. I can stay like this for hours if I need to. You cannot hurt yourself."

I cried. I wanted to badly to kill myself. The urge was stronger than it had ever been before. With each depression my reason for killing myself became more and more justified and reasonable. I sobbed as he held me down. He continued to talk to me and tell me all the hundreds of reasons why I needed to be alive. Our three children being at the top of the list. I sobbed as he told me to imagine their reaction when they find out Mommy had died. I sobbed when he told me about our daughter's future wedding and my chair being empty. I sobbed as he told me about graduations I would miss out on and grandchildren I would never meet. His reasons were good reasons. I stopped struggling so much. But he still held me. For hours, he held me to protect me from myself. When I had to pee, he followed me to the bathroom and watched me. Once he let me go, he escorted me through the house. He dispensed my medication but hid the rest. He hid all the kitchen knives in an unknown location.

After that depressive episode had passed a few weeks later, he talked to me about it. He told me that he did what he had to do because he loves me. But he couldn't promise he can do that again next time. The children were gone, but what would happen if it happened again and they were home, or he was at work? We decided that if it were to happen again, we would seek out options. There had to be something that would help me.

Chapter 4
They're going to send me away

I was 30. My husband had unexpectedly lost his job. We sat on our porch, stunned. Already living paycheck-to-paycheck, we knew that we would lose our house. We knew our life was about to change dramatically.

My parents were very sympathetic of our situation. They offered us to move in with them until we got back on our feet. With really no other options, we accepted their offer. At the time I felt this would be a good move. I thought my parents could help with our children and they could help my husband who seemed overwhelmed as my condition seemed to be worsening each episode. I thought it would help our family.

One evening, I stood in the garage as my husband sorted laundry. I stood and watched him sort the clothes by color, and I just watched. "What's wrong," he asked.

"I just. It's just." I couldn't explain it. My bipolar felt like I had a rash on my leg. And our current situation of living with them felt like I was wearing a pair of pants that was irritating the rash.

My mom walked into the garage, followed by my dad.

"Family meeting?" my mom asked and laughed, unaware of how I was feeling.

So I broke. The tears began to flow and I covered my face. What had began as laundry sorting ending up being a meeting.

"I'm so sorry," I said. "I'm so sorry that you have to see me like this. I'm so sorry that you have to deal with me. Sometimes it gets so bad that I can't get out of bed. Mike handles everything because I just can't. Sometimes it gets so bad that I can't shower and I can't function and I am so sorry."

My mother began to tear up.

"It's okay," she said. "You wouldn't apologize if you had diabetes. We support you. We love you. You are our child and we will always support you."

My heart swelled. This was the first time they talked to me about my "issues". They told me they supported me! They told me they loved me! I went to bed that night with a weight off my shoulders. I had always thought that my mom didn't believe me. I had always thought that she thought I was making it up for attention or out of boredom. And that night she supported me. Her words meant the world to me.

But immediately upon move-in, the depression hit. I cried myself to sleep every night. We had lost our freedom. But most of all, I had lost my routine that kept me partly sane. I had lost my "job" of keeping a household up and running. I lost my purpose. I lost my reason for existing. I became a hermit to our bedroom, only coming out to eat and pee. The depression continued and with each day it grew worse.

One day, a few weeks after we had moved in, the depression became too much. I was deeply suicidal, much more than usual. I whispered my thoughts of death to my husband and he listened.

"I just feel like you will be better off without me," I said.

"I won't. I would be devastated." he said.

"I can't do this anymore. I don't want to do this anymore. I think I need to go to the crisis center." I whispered.

He agreed. I put my medication in a ziploc bag, emptied my pockets and followed him to the truck. The drive there was silent. I hoped they allowed smoking. I didn't know what to expect.

When we arrived, we had to knock on a screened off metal door. Someone from the inside unlocked the door, opened the door, and then relocked the door.

"Hello," a man said from a desk. "What brings you to us today?"
I stayed silent. I didn't know what to say. I didn't know what I should say.
"My wife is suicidal," my husband chimed in. The man pulled out a notebook and began to jot down notes.
"Can you elaborate on this?" the man at the desk asked me.
"Well I...I feel suicidal. I want to kill myself." I said it. Outloud.
"How? What are your plans?" the man asked.
"Well," I thought. "I was thinking about sitting in front of a train. Or slitting my wrists. Or taking my dad's pain pills. He has a huge bottle of them for his legs."
"I see," the man said. "Okay, it seems that you are a danger to yourself so we are going to hold you."
"Do I leave now?" my husband asked.
"Yes, she will let you out" and the man gestured towards a woman sitting at another desk.
I looked at my husband and I wanted to go with him. I knew I would be held in some sort of way, but seeing him in that moment, I wanted him to stay. Or I wanted to go. But instead the door was unlocked, he kissed my forehead, walked out, and the door was relocked.
We went over my name, insurance, medications, who I was seeing for mental health, my diagnosis, my symptoms and my suicidal plans.
"Okay, there is a mandatory 23 hour hold. After that a doctor will see you and they will determine if you need to be admitted or not. You will stay up here with us, just let us know if you need anything. There is an empty bed in this room," he pointed to a door right next to me "and there is a tv in there too."
Twenty three hours? Are you kidding me? I opened the door to the room and found two white beds, a boxed in television and a small square table. One of the beds had a hole punched in the wall above it. I decided to sit on the other bed. As I sat down the springs screeched and the bed nearly folded in half. Twenty three hours.
I glanced at my phone, my only source of the time. It was 2:30 and my phone was at 54%. I felt like smoking.

"Excuse me", I said as I poked my head out the door. "Can I smoke?"

"Sorry," the man at the desk said. "This is a non-smoking facility. We use nicotine patches but it's too late to give you one. I can give you one in the morning."

"Ok" I said and returned to sitting on the cot.

For about an hour I sat indian style on the cot. I felt like I was waiting for something. A doctor to come in. A therapist to come in. But soon I realized, no one was coming. Instead, I had to wait out the 23 hour time period before seeing anyone.

"Here, let me turn this on for you" the man at the desk said as he entered the dark and quiet room. Soon, the television came to life. He handed me the remote. I scrolled through the channels and found The Sisterhood of the Traveling Pants. I decided to crawl under the blanket so I kicked off my shoes and pulled back the cotton blanket and white sheet. When I layed in the bed and covered up, I realized the pillow was made out of plastic. My head and feet were elevated, my butt sunk into a hole. I watched the movie. A few hours passed. Dinner was served. It was a paper plate of spaghetti, cheap salad and mixed veggies with a small carton of milk. I hate milk. I didn't eat. I just left it sitting on the table. More hours passed. I couldn't watch tv anymore. I began to weep. I bawled. I wanted to go home. I couldn't sit in this room for 23 hours. I couldn't just lay in this bed for an entire day. There had to be another way to see a doctor than laying in this awful bed for an entire day. I bawled and gasped for air. My phone was nearly dead. The time was 8:30 p.m.

"Excuse me" I said as I stood at the opening of the door, my face wet from tears that still fell. "Can I go home?" I wiped away my tears as more fell.

"Uhm, what do you mean?" the man at the desk asked.

"I want to go home. Sitting here," I gestured to the room, "is just making me feel worse. I can't sit in there alone for an entire day. I want to go home. I want my husband."

"We really advise that you stay, you can see a doctor after the 23 hours have passed." he said.

"But I feel better." I lied.

"You feel better?" he asked.

"Yes, I feel better and staying here is making me feel worse, I want to go home to my husband." I sobbed

"Okay okay, let me call the on-call doctor and see what they say." he said.

I returned to my room. I didn't understand why I couldn't just leave. I came in voluntarily.

After a while I was called back into the office. The doctor had decided that I could leave as long as my husband could confirm that the pain pills were moved and there were no weapons in the home. I called him on the landline phone and he spoke with the man at the desk. My husband sounded irritated that he had to come pick me up after 9 o'clock at night, which I understood, but I didn't care. I was going home! I sat impatiently on the cot until I heard him come in. He again confirmed that the pills had been locked up and there were no weapons in the home. The man at the desk gave me back my purse and medications, and unlocked the door for us. I was going home. And I was NEVER going back there.

A few weeks later, on a Friday, I laid on the bed on my stomach, sprawled out across the sheets and blankets. My chin rested on a pillow. I didn't want to mess up my hair. I watched the bunny in her cage run from the first floor to the second and back again. I wondered if he would remember to change her litter box. I know he would remember to feed her, but I usually change her litter box. I decided the kids would adjust. Maybe they would have to seek therapy. Maybe they would be young enough that they wouldn't remember me. I would just be a box of pictures and second-hand memories. That would be better. I didn't want them to remember me. Especially like this.

I got up from the bed and sat at the foot of the bed. I had 45 minutes until my therapy appointment. I already knew what I was going to say. I knew I was going to tell her that I didn't care anymore. Before, the thought of my family losing me is what kept me from killing myself. The trauma of finding my body would be too much for them.

But I had thought of a few ways that would prevent them from finding me. There were strong trees in the woods. There were a lot of trains in town. I would feel bad for the conductor. I'm sure it would be a bad day for him, but how else would I do it? I know the best way is to swallow a whole bottle of pills. We happened to have hundreds of Vicodin in a pill bottle in my parents bathroom. I could easily swallow them all and chase it with a few glasses of wine. But then I would leave a mess. I would vomit. And my body would be lying somewhere. There would be a mess. I didn't want a mess. I wanted to just disappear. I wanted to not exist anymore. Ideally, a guardian angel in search of it's wings would float down and show me my life if I had not existed at all, like It's A Wonderful Life. That would be perfect.

I haven't found an angel yet, and I haven't come up with a way to completely disappear. I have thought about driving away and never coming back but where would I go? All I knew is that my family deserved better. My husband deserved a better wife. He got a lemon. My kids deserved a better mom. I was broken and they deserved better. By going away, I would cut the chain that was connecting them to the burden of me.

I know my death would be painful for them. But they would adjust. They would be okay. I just couldn't do it anymore. I couldn't live this life anymore. I felt like I was dying from the inside out, the way a sausage in the microwave cooks too much on the inside and becomes dry and tough. I had become a shell of emptiness. My family deserved better. And I was going to give them the opportunity to have better. I would be replaced by someone unbroken. Not a lemon. Someone that could fully be there for them in the ways that I couldn't.

It was time to leave for my appointment. I whispered to my husband "I'm having a very bad day".

"I know", he said. He hugged me.

"They're going to send me away", I said. My voice was shaking.

"If they do, that's ok. I love you."

I didn't say it back. I always say it back, but I couldn't.

I climbed into the truck. My watch beeped for 3:00. I remembered to bring it this time. The last time I went to the crisis center, there were no clocks and it drove me crazy. I remembered to grab it this time. I just had to know the time. I had to know how much time had passed.

The wait was fast, and my therapist was chatty at first. She asked me about a recent support group I attended. I brushed over the subject and she instantly knew something was wrong.

"I can't do this", I said as I began to cry.

"Do what?", she asked.

"I can't do this anymore. I feel like I'm dying. I can't bear to look at my children. I can't keep living anymore. It hurts too much."

"Are you feeling suicidal right now?"

I sobbed. "Yes"

"Do you have a plan?" She asked. They always ask that question.

"Which plan? I have ten."

She sat silently for a few moments. "I'm going to call in a crisis counselor, is that ok?"

I nodded.

A few minutes later, a man arrived. He introduced himself and then kneeled down to try to make eye contact with me. The tunnel vision had taken hold and my glossed over gaze was fixated on the book shelf. I couldn't move anymore. I was frozen.

"Sarah, I am here to help you. I want to first of all say thank you, and great job for coming to us. That is absolutely fantastic. You should be proud of yourself."

I didn't feel proud at all. I didn't feel anything.

"Now, tell me, do you have family?"

"Yes, 3 kids", I whispered.

"Your children need you. I know you don't feel that way right now, but they need you. Sarah, tell me your plans."

I whispered. "A train. A rope on a tree. The pills. A knife. Anything." The man sighed and dropped his head.

"Sarah, I believe you are in a crisis right now and I would like to escort you to the crisis center to get help. Is that ok?"

I whispered again, still fixated on the book shelf. "Yes. But can I smoke first?"

"Absolutely", he said. "I'm going to go pull the car around because it's raining pretty good.

My therapist walked with me down the sidewalk and to the ashtray near the parking lot. I smoked. I knew it would be the last. The last time I was at the crisis center, they said there was no smoking in the facility and it was too late for a nicotine patch. I took long drags, and then apologized as I put it out in the ashtray.

The three of us climbed into the car. The rain drenched my hair. It rained the way I felt.

We arrived at the crisis center. The door was unlocked, and then relocked once we were inside. Hearing the lock on the door click over hurt my ears. I was locked in. The receptionist asked if I wanted to talk. I was done talking about it. I didn't want to talk about it anymore. The therapists relayed the information to the receptionist. They told her about my numerous plans. They told her I was in a serious crisis and would need to be admitted. I stared at the floor as they talked. The last time I was here, I counted the tiles. I didn't feel like counting this time. I just stared.

After a while, the therapists left. I was locked in. They showed me to a crisis room. The same cot I remembered from the last time. Within minutes, a sweet nurse came in with a cup. A pill to help me calm down, and a nicotine patch. "Thank god", I thought. Nothing is worse than being in crisis while simultaneously being forced to quit smoking. I wanted to chain smoke at this point.

The last time I was here, nothing happened. No one came to check on me. No meds were administered. No nicotine patch was given. I sat in the room, alone, weeping, for hours. After 8 hours, I begged to go home. I pleaded. I told them I felt better (I lied) but I knew that going home to my loving husband would make me feel better than sobbing on a cot for hours on end.

This time was different. I could tell by the immense amount of paperwork at the desk. I could tell by the phone calls. I took off my shoes, curled up in fetal position on the bed and just stared.

"Would you like a blanket sweetie?" The nurse asked when she came in to check on me.

"Yes please."I said, still staring into oblivion.

She covered me with a warm blanket and I drifted to sleep.

"Sarah?" My name being called startled me. I had no idea where I was or what time it was. "You're being transferred to a Psychiatric hospital in Sacramento. An ambulance will be transporting you."

"Ok", I mumbled in my half-awake state. I drifted back asleep.

"Sarah?" I again woke up startled and disoriented. "The ambulance is here to transport you."

I sat up in the bed. Whatever med they had given me had made the room spin in one direction and my head spin in the other direction. I stumbled putting my shoes on, gathered my jacket and walked towards the door.

The rain continued to pour down in sheets. It matched my mood. "Watch your head", the ambulance driver warned me as I stepped into the ambulance. To the left was a bed. To the right was a bench. I didn't know where to go, so I just stood there in a daze.

"Have a seat", the female ambulance attendant said as she pointed to the bed. I sat down. And then laid down. I was so tired. She buckled three seat belts across me. "Let me get you a blanket." She said, and she wrapped me in the warmest blanket I've ever felt. It felt wonderful.

"I love your shoes." She said, pointing to my sparkly red slippers I was wearing. "They're just like dorothy's shoes from the wizard of oz," she said and smiled. "Ruby red slippers."

"Thank you," I said as I closed my eyes.

"It's a two hour drive so feel free to get some rest. It's going to be a long drive." I had already started to drift to sleep.

Every now and then a bump or jolt would startle me awake and I would watch the street lights passing backwards through the window. I looked around the ambulance a few times. The shelves that contained the medical supplies were zip tied closed. I couldn't move because of the seat belts and I wasn't sure if they were for safety or to restrain me. Probably both.

After two hours, the ambulance came to a stop and the back doors opened. We had arrived. I wasn't sure if I was to walk or stay on the gurney but before I could ask they pulled the gurney out of the ambulance, the wheels came down and they began to wheel me to the front door.

The front doors were locked. It was 4 o'clock in the morning. The ambulance driver buzzed the doorbell and after a few minutes someone came down to open the door. We were directed to the elevators which had to be unlocked. The nurse pressed "3" on the elevator panel and up we went.

Once we arrived in the lobby of floor 3, a nurse was seated on a leather couch opposite of another leather couch. "Have a seat", he said. I was removed from the gurney and I sat on the couch. Then, the questions started.

How are you feeling?
Do you feel suicidal?
Sign here.
Initial here.
Have you attempted suicide in the past?
What is your diagnosis?
What medications are you taking?

"You are lucky", the nurse said at the end of the interview. "This wing is strictly for mood disorders. Bipolar. It was created two years ago. You're lucky."

He lead me to a room where a single cot lay in the middle of the empty room and a hospital gown laid on the bed. "Undress and I will get a female nurse to do a skin check" he said as he left the room. I removed my clothes and put the gown on. I was unsure if I was supposed to leave my underwear on, so I did anyways.

The female nurse arrived and she examined my body. She checked the crevices for hidden weapons, my wrists and legs to see if I had harmed myself. She opened my buttocks to see if I had hidden something there.

After the examination, she gave me another hospital gown to drape over the back like a robe. She walked me to the entrance of the third floor where she scanned her ID badge and the door clicked open.

We walked down the hall a ways and she pointed to a room. "This is your room."

My name was written on the door along with another name; Molly. "Freaking great", I thought. A roommate. All I wanted was to be left alone. As I walked into the room I saw the simplicity of it. Two beds, two book shelves. All the corners were rounded. The windows were sealed off and covered in hard plastic. A bathroom was also present however the "door" was a simple curtain.

I noticed Molly's hair was purple, just like mine. I didn't care though. I didn't care about anything. All I cared about was sleeping. I pulled the blankets back and crawled into the empty bed. I curled up into fetal position and cried. And cried. And cried. And cried. And cried. For 26 hours, I cried. I didn't move. I didn't pee. I didn't eat. I refused interactions. I refused everything. I cried. And I cried. And I cried. I considered bashing my head against the footboard of the bed. I considered chewing off the strings on the hospital gown and tying them around my neck. I considered putting my head in the toilet and drowning myself. Instead, I cried for 26 hours, and a nurse checked on me every 15 minutes.

At one point, a nurse arrived in my room and asked if I wanted my clothes washed. Clean clothes and a shower sounded nice so I said yes. She took them and put them in a bag outside the door. I went back to sleep.

I woke up starving. I didn't know what day it was but thanks to good planning on my part, I was wearing a wrist watch. It had been two days. A nurse walked into the room and said, "Sarah, your dinner is in the day room," and he left just as quickly as he came in. "Great," I thought. "They are manipulating me out of the bed with food." I sighed and complied, slipping my ruby red slippers on, wrapping the outer gown tightly around myself and I shuffled to the "day room". Inside I found people. Patients like me. A table with puzzles, a tv. Books. Coloring books. A table with pitchers of juice and coffee, and my to-go box of food with my name written on it. I grabbed the box and headed towards my room but a sign above the door read "No food or drinks in the

bedrooms" stopped me. So I found an empty chair, opened the container, and ate whatever it was that was there. I didn't care.

The other patients talked. They laughed. They made jokes, played cards, read books. I hated them. I loathed them. How could they laugh at a time like this? How could they casually be reading a book as if nothing catastrophic had happened.

A girl seated at the table reading a book talked to my roommate. Their conversation had been going on for a while because both had set the books down, but I overheard "Yeah, I waited until everyone was gone. My sister came home early from school so I had to wait. But once everyone was gone, it was bottoms up." She said and chuckled. "That's why I'm here." Her arms and hands were covered in dozens and dozens of self-inflicted scars. There were burn marks too. I flinched.

I ate the dinner and while I was finishing up, a nurse yelled "Group time!" Down the hall. The remaining patients filled in and sat down in the empty chairs. "Welp", I thought, "I guess I'll be attending my first group."

The nurse heading the group asked everyone to go around the room and state their name, their "mood number on a scale of 0 to 10" and what their goal was for the day as well as what they would wish for if they had a magic lamp. I didn't volunteer to talk, I hoped they would forget about me. But they didn't. "Sarah? How about you?" She asked.

"Hi, I'm Sarah. My mood is at a..... 1. I would wish that my ruby red slippers actually worked. And my goal today was to shower." The nurse thanked me for sharing and the group moved on to the topic. It was dealing with anxiety. A worksheet was passed out and it listed the symptoms of anxiety. We took turns reading the paragraphs on the handout. Then the group was over. I sat in the hospital gown in the chair where I had ate my dinner and I didn't know what to do.

I decided to hunt my clothes down. The nurse had put them out for laundry at 11:30. It was now 6:30. Surely they should be done by now. I stood up and headed towards the hall. I found a nurse sitting in a chair filling out paperwork. "Excuse me", I said. "A nurse took my clothes this morning to be washed and I was wondering if they have been cleaned." She asked me for a description of the clothes and then headed towards the laundry room in the other wing.

I went back and laid on the bed.

I clicked my heels together three times. "There's no place like home. There's no place like home. There's no place like home." It didn't work. I was still laying on the bed in a hospital gown wearing my ruby red slippers that were broken. I was broken.

A few hours passed and the evening meds were passed out. The little cups they used to hand out meds reminded me of the little cups they had at fast food restaurants for ketchup. I swallowed my meds and then asked about my clothes again. The nurse responded that they were in the dryer and were not dry yet so I would probably get them back in the morning.

"Sarah?" I rolled over and saw a nurse. "Good morning. The doctor would like to see you now." I jumped up from the bed and headed towards the hall. The nurse opened the door and lead me to a small room.

A man sat in a chair with a portable laptop and what appeared to be a file. My file. "Sarah?", he asked. "Yes, that's me."

"Have a seat", he said. He opened my file. "I like your shoes. Ruby Red slippers. My daughter would love them. So what happened? How did you end up here?"

I told him about the meeting with the therapist, the ambulance ride, the urges to bash my head into the footboard of the bed.

"And your diagnosis says bipolar? Can you emphasize on that a little bit?"

"Well," I said, "I have my lows. That's pretty obvious. I get suicidal a lot. I usually fight it off, but this time I couldn't. But I also have these

highs. It feels like intermittent ADHD. I get really creative and hyper.
I get so hyper. My legs bounce and I start jumping up and down. I
can't sleep for days. Once I decided to start a business. Another
time I decided to write a book. I became devoted to those projects. I
barely ate. I didn't sleep. And then after a few days, I crashed back
down into depression. These highs feel like I have butterflies under
my skin. Like I just can't calm down. I just can't settle down."
The doctor nodded and said "Type II then? That's certainly what it
sounds like."
We discussed my medications, he added a new one, upped the
dosage of another, and the frequency of another. Then the
appointment was over and I was lead back to my room. But I was
still wearing the hospital gown.
I went to the desk at the front of the hall and spoke through the
small slit in the window.
"Excuse me," I said. "My clothes were sent to laundry yesterday
morning and I still haven't gotten them back yet. They were
supposed to be in the dryer."
A nurse with dark hair said she would go check. I went back to my
room.
About 10 minutes later she arrived at my room with an armful of
clothes. She handed them to me but I didn't take them. "These
aren't mine", I said. "These are men's clothes."
"Oh", she said. "What did yours look like?" She asked. I described
them again.
"Oh my gosh." She said and shook her head. "This is ridiculous.
Your clothes have to be around here somewhere."
I laid back on the bed. "Group time! Group!" A nurse called down the
hall, so I stood up and went back into the day room where we
discussed the symptoms of depression and why suicide is not the
answer.

While discussing our mood number, a curly haired tall man asked "Hey, can ya'll open a window in here or something? It's stuffy." he paused. "I promise I won't jump out". The room erupted with laughter. I laughed too.

Later, a nurse came into my room, "Sarah, did your shirt have a print on it?" Puzzled, I answered "Yes, unicorns." The nurse shook her head. "Okay, I'm going to need you to come with me." I followed her through the locked doors and into the other wing of the floor. We passed by a few rooms and then we stopped at a room. The door was ajar.

"Loretta," the nurse said. "Those are not your clothes."

A middle aged woman with wiry hair and glazed over eyes stood wearing my two shirts I was missing and my sweater.

"But ya'll owe me a pair of pants." Loretta said and placed her hands on her hips.

The nurse sighed. "Loretta, those are not your clothes. Those are Sarah's clothes. Please take them off."

"Well ya'll owe me pants!" She shouted as we left her room. The nurse said she would rewash my clothes and then hopefully, return them to me.

I got my clothes back. I saw the doctor three times. I talked to the nurses and I joined in the groups more. I started to go down with everyone else to the cafeteria for breakfast lunch and dinner. The cafeteria held about a dozen round tables with six chairs at each table, all of them vacant. The vacancy of the cafeteria matched the vacancy of the rest of the hospital. There was no one in the halls, no nurses in the elevators, no one in the lobby. Everyone was behind locked doors.

While standing in the short line to get dinner, I looked through the large glass window and saw a small babbling creek. From the left, a small duck appeared and it waddled to the creek and stepped in. I began to cry because I wished I was the duck. I wanted to feel the water and the sun and the wind. I missed the world.

As the days passed, I found myself laughing at jokes. I started to read a book. I started to color in a coloring book.

A few days in, I was comfortably sitting in a chair in the hall reading a book I was 300 pages into when a new patient walked in. She wore a hospital gown. Her head was down. Her hair was chaotic. Her face was streaming with tears. Her eyes were glazed over.

I knew her.

She was me.

I had been her when I first came in. I had hated the laughter. I had hated the girl sitting in the hall casually reading a book as if nothing catastrophic had just happened. I had wanted to scream too.

I didn't make eye contact. I didn't even say hello because I know that she wouldn't have wanted me to. I wouldn't have wanted that. After a few days, she came out of her room and joined the groups, just like I had. She showered and put on her clothes. She laughed. She ate. She healed.

She healed just like I had.

When I was finally released, I stepped outside the doors and into the fresh air for the first time in what felt like years.

I cried. The cold wind touched my face and I cried because I missed the wind. And the trees. And the rain. And the dirt. And the clouds. I had healed.

I felt at an "8" when I left. I believed that I had healed completely. That by seeing the full spectrum of bipolar disorder, I understood more thus, I had healed.

But three weeks later, the depression returned, as it always does, as it always has, as it always will. With my new knowledge from the hospital, I willed myself to make it through the storm. But each bought of depression pulled me further downwards. Our current situation (unemployment and living with my parents) agitated my depression.

I tried to color in an adult coloring book one day. The bed was made, the house was clean, and I was alone. So I colored. But somewhere between a rose petal and a blade of grass I dismantled a pencil sharpener. Easily, I was able to release the screw that held the razor blade and in my hand I had a small razorblade which I stared at for a few minutes.

I walked to the bathroom, pulled down my pants and sat on the toilet let. I held the razor blade in my hand and I closed my eyes. I opened my eyes and I knew what I wanted to do. I had wanted to do it for years. Slowly, I dragged the razor blade across my right thigh. Blood began to dribble out of the cuts. With each cut I became more daring and made them longer and longer. There were fifteen cuts total, and the blood began to drip down my leg. I wadded up some toilet paper and put it on the cuts. I felt so relieved. I felt so complete. I felt so content.

I pulled my pants up but some blood began to seep through, so I folded some toilet paper into a square, put it on the cuts, and pulled my pants up.

I returned to the coloring book and soon, my husband, father and son came home. I could hear them talking and laughing in the kitchen. They didn't know my secret.

I continued to color. My husband came in the room with a smile on his face.

"Hello," he said. "Coloring?"

"Yeah," I said and shrugged my shoulders.

He came over and kissed my forehead.

"What's that?" he asked as he pointed to the few red droplets of blood on my jeans.

"I don't know. Nothing." I said.

"Alright, well, I'm gonna go out and mow the lawn but I will come check on you in a little bit." he said as he put his yard work shoes on.

Before he left, he stopped.

"Are you okay?" he asked.

"No," I said. "I'm having a bad day. A very bad day."

"Okay, I will come check on you when I'm done." he said.

Once he left I put the coloring book away and wrapped into my blanket burrito. I wanted to cut myself again. I wanted to burn myself. I wanted to throw myself out of a moving car. I wanted to drown myself. I wanted to sit on the train tracks and wait for a train. These thoughts swirled around in my head over and over again. I continued to make plans and think of ways to kill myself. That's all I was thinking about in my burrito.

After a while, he came to check on me.

"What's wrong?" he asked.

"Everything." I said.

"What do you mean?" he asked.

"I just… I want to kill myself. I can't do this anymore." I began to cry.

"Dammit Sarah, not this again. You know what's gonna happen if I take you back there. You're gonna call me crying in a few hours and I will have to go back to pick you up." he said angrily.

"Not this time!" I said "This time I won't come home. I really need to go."

"Why don't you just take a nap? Maybe that will make you feel better." he said.

"There's something else," I said and looked away.

I pulled the blanket back, unzipped my jeans and removed the toilet paper.

"Holy shit Sarah. What the fuck?" he stammered.

I pulled my pants back up and rolled over. He left the room. Soon, he came back.

"Your mom is coming home from work early. She is going to try to talk me out of taking you to the hospital, I just know it. But we have got to get you to the hospital." He said. He must have called her and told her. He left the room again. I heard my mom's truck pull into the driveway.

I pulled the blankets over my head.

I heard a small knock at the door and a "Hello" from my mother.

"Come in", I said and put the blankets back over my head.

She walked next to my bed and stood next to me as I lay under the blankets. She grabbed the top blanket and tore it off, leaving me with the sheet.

"Oh no, we are not doing this. You can't just lay here in this bed all day long Sarah. You have got to get up and get on with your life. What kind of childhood are your children having? What kind of a wife are you being? Your daughters should be sent to their biological father's house if this is how you are going to behave. And the cutting, what are you, twelve? Do we have to stand outside the door while you shower now? Jesus! Get your ass out of bed and deal with it. You don't even get out of bed anymore, you aren't even trying. And why is it so bad now? If you've had these...issues... all your life, then why is it so bad now? And you can't go running off to the god damn hospital every time you have a bad day. And why won't your doctors tell us anything?"

I sobbed into the sheet. I pointed to the small printout of phone numbers and names hanging on the wall.

"Call them," I said in between sobs.

"For what? They think I beat you or something. They're all full of shit. You aren't going to that damn hospital, you need to put on your

big girl panties and deal with this. Be a mom. Be a wife. Grow up."
and she left the room.

And in that moment, in between sobs, my heart sunk to the floor and
shattered into a million little pieces. The suicidal justifications in my
head had been vocalized by my mother. I wanted to end my life
because I was a bad mom and a bad wife, and she just told me that
I was.

I sobbed and sobbed. My relationship with my mother was at this
point broken, unfixable, forever tarnished beyond repair. That
moment left ruins of burned bridges and a scorched heart. My heart.
My husband returned to the room.

"I don't give a fuck what your mom thinks, I'm taking you to the
hospital." he said. "You need to go to the hospital, it's obvious. You
cut yourself!" he gestured to my leg. "Pack a bag, we are leaving."
He left the room. I heard whispers in the kitchen.

He returned to the room.

"Your mom just fucking told me that I need to take our son and go to
my dad's for the weekend. I'm not leaving you! You are my wife!
You are my family! I'm not going anywhere." he shouted. He left the
room again.

My mother entered the room again.

"You aren't running off the hospital again. You need to get out of
bed and deal with this. Dinner is on the table." she said and left the
room.

I didn't eat dinner. I remained in bed for the evening. I ended up not
going to the crisis center that night, but I should have. There have
been many days that I should have gone to the crisis center, but I
didn't. The crisis center is there to protect me from myself and
whether I go 5 times or 500 times, the door is always open (kind of)
and I will always be helped. I should have gone that day, but I didn't.
Instead, my relationship with my mother was forever bruised.

Four weeks later I found myself back at the crisis center.

"Hello", the attendant said. "Why are you here today?"

I told her about my ideas of hanging myself, sitting in front of a train, slitting my wrists, anything really. I was desperate for death.

"Alright," she said. "Looks like you will be admitted. And we have plenty of room here so you will be staying here"

I was a little curious as to how this hospital operated as before I went to the other hospital two hours away. I looked forward to the groups and all the help I would receive. After answering their questions, I was instructed to go lay down on the cot as before.

I layed down and went to sleep. I knew the drill. I had to be in the room for 23 hours before I would be admitted. So I spent most of this time sleeping. Sleep seemed to help. After the 23 hours of sleeping I actually felt better, but I still was admitted.

A nurse came and got me and led me through a door I had never been through before. It opened up into a large room that seemed to include a small living room, a small dining area, a small kitchen and a small courtyard.

I sat down at a desk and the nurse examined my mental state and my vital signs. Afterwards I was assigned to a room. She explained that the bedrooms were locked until 2pm. I didn't know what to do with myself so I stood there. A large sign yelled out on the wall "STAY BEHIND THE RED LINE" and on the ground was a red line that kept the patients away from the nurses station. I felt like I was in jail. I felt like I had a developmental disability. On a whiteboard a schedule for the day was listed out. From 12:00 to 1:00 it was "Music and walking". I didn't feel like walking. No one else was walking. And there was no music playing.

So I sat on a couch and watched the news. There was no remote and it was in a clear plastic box. Finally at 2:00pm, they unlocked the bedroom doors. I went into my bedroom and saw there were three cots. The beds were hard, and had a plastic mattress about 2 inches thick. I sat cross legged on the bed and began to read a book, the only book they had in the book shelf. About ten pages in, a man walked into the room. He began to dig through a table. I was unsure of if he was my roommate so I asked him. He didn't respond. He had a blanket draped over him. He then walked to my table and picked up my shirt. He sniffed it. He picked up my underwear. He sniffed them.

"Excuse me!" I shouted.

He ignored me.

"Excuse me, those are mine!" I shouted.

He ignored me.

He walked across the room and sat on a cot and stared at me. I stared back. I was terrified.

Shortly after, a nurse came in and ordered him to leave the room. It was a female room and he was not allowed in there.

Later, when I was sitting on the couch again, I considered taking a shower. But down the hall I heard a commotion. One of the patients was continuously opening the shower door on a female patient. The door did not have a lock.

Nevermind.

This hospital felt disgusting.

I wanted to go home so badly. I told the nurses I felt fine, I was ready to go home. I was the highest functioning patient in the hospital. No one else was even capable of holding a conversation. Most of them had glazed over eyes and mumbled to themselves. I had to get out of there.

The following morning the doctor saw me. I explained that I felt fine. It was truly the initial sleeping for 23 hours that had helped me. After other questions, she decided to release me.

A few hours later I was released and my husband picked me up. I didn't feel the "8" I had felt before. There were no groups to learn from. There was no learning experience to be thankful for. The only thing that I had learned was that I would never, ever return to that hospital no matter what.

As he drove me home I sat in silence. What a waste of time it was. But I guess if the hospital's purpose was to keep me from harming myself then it had succeeded. But it had failed me in so many other ways. The experience was not the useful and purposeful experience I had had before. It was a useless jail that made me feel violated.

Three weeks later I was sitting in my therapist's office. I had my watch in my purse. I knew where I was going. I told her I just couldn't go on anymore. I told her of my numerous plans. I was done with living. She offered to walk me to the crisis center across the street.

The door was unlocked from the inside, we were allowed in, and then the door was relocked.

"What brings you to us today?" the man behind the desk said.

I noticed a woman sitting in a chair. Her hair looked fried. Her skin was wrinkled. She looked tired. Great, I thought, I have to spill my guts in front of another patient.

"Hello," she said. "I'm a doctor here."

"Oh," I said surprised.

I told the man behind the desk my numerous plans, he jotted them down in his notebook.

"Let me see her chart," the Doctor asked. A woman at another desk handed her a folder with my name on it. The doctor scanned through the pages.

"What meds are you taking sweetie?" she asked.

I listed out the four medications I was taking, at what dosage and how often.

The doctor covered her face.

"Oh my," she said. "There's a lot that needs to happen."

She looked at the man behind the desk and told him to up this medication, change that medication to bedtime, increase that medication and so on.

Then she turned to me.

"I'm also going to put you on Lithium. A low dose though.None of these meds will do anything for suicidal thoughts but a low dose of lithium is proven to decrease suicidal thoughts." she said.

"Add 300 milligrams of lithium, starting tonight." she said to the man behind the desk.

"Okay," I said. "But I have a question. If I am admitted, can I go somewhere else?" I asked.

"No," the man said. "That's not how it works. We have room here for you. If you went somewhere else before it was because we were full. But we have room today. Why?" he asked.

"I just can't go back there. I refuse." I said.

"Why?" asked the doctor.

"I was violated back there" I told them. And I told them of the man that came into my room who sniffed my underwear and of the girl trying to shower while another man kept watching her.

"Okay" the doctor said. "Stay here overnight, let's make sure these med adjustments are okay and I will see you in the morning and we will likely release you tomorrow."

"You're very lucky," the man behind the desk said. "That never happens. People don't see a doctor until they have been admitted for a few days."

I was shown my room. The same white cot from the times before. I put my wristwatch on. I sat on the cot.

"Want a taco?" a woman asked who was sitting on a cot across the room from mine. "My husband brought them and there's an extra."

"It's okay," I said. "No thankyou" I hugged my knees.

She walked over and handed me the fast food bag.

"Here ya go. It's good" she said and smiled.

"Thanks" I said.

I ate the taco and it was good. I felt more at ease this time. I had already seen the doctor and my meds were already adjusted. I just had to wait out until I saw the doctor again to release me. So we watched episode after episode of Storage Wars and I fell asleep soundly.

I woke up the next morning anxious to leave. I asked the man behind the desk when the doctor usually comes in. He said about 10ish. Ten o'clock came and went and there was no doctor. At 11:30 I asked again. He said she had just arrived, there was one patient before me, but she would see me soon. I sat in the office this time, refusing to go sit on the cot. I drummed my fingers on the chair and tapped my feet. I was anxious to go home.

Finally the doctor came in and she sat down next to me in the seat she had sat in the day before. I felt bad for mistaking her for a patient, but she had definitely lead a rough life judging by her hair and skin.

"Okay," she said after reviewing notes made in my file. "It seems you are okay and ready to go home, alright?" she said.

I grinned. "Yes, I am ready to go home."

I phoned my husband from the landline phone and he came shortly after to pick me up.

Chapter 6
Relief

The water glistens in the sun. Shimmering sunlight bounces off the bottom of the pool. The water was cold when I first got in but now it feels refreshing. With each stroke, my hands glide into the water and propels my body forward. Left arm, right arm. Breathe. Left arm, right arm. Breathe. My goggles have fogged up proving wrong the "Fog Proof!" proclamation on the packaging when I bought them. The water surrounds my body, tiny air bubbles form at my fingertips as I swim. My legs kick continuously, like a propeller on a boat. As I approach the wall I take a deep breathe and dive forward into a ball. I untwist, kick off, and streamline towards my next lap. Left arm, right arm. Breathe. Kick kick kick kick kick. Left arm, right arm. Breathe.

I'm the only one in my lane, but not the only one in the pool. College kids are at the far end of the pool swimming laps. Their chiseled chests and speedos hint that they belong to the swim team. Pop music plays on a stereo. I'm unsure of the purpose of the radio considering our heads are underwater 90% of the time, but whatever. In the other lanes are swimmers like me, Lap Swimmers. We are all a part of a program hosted by the college. Monday, Wednesday and Friday we swim at 5am, noon, and 5pm. Some swim only one session, while others swim multiple sessions. When I am hypomanic, I swim all three. If I am depressed, I swim none. I try to go 4-6 times a week.

Right arm, left arm, right arm, left arm. Breathe. My lungs feel like they are going to burst. I try for six strokes before breathing next. Next to me is a middle aged man with a horseshoe receding hairline. Next to him is a man in a scuba outfit, complete with a face mask and snorkel. I call him Scuba Steve. Then there is Janet with her sun visor on as she uses the kickboard like she always does. The rest, I don't know. We say hello to each other when we arrive, we say goodbye when we leave, but we never talk amongst ourselves. We are there for one purpose only and that is to swim. The clock reads 25:08. I groan. I want to get out. My legs hurt and I am ready to get out, but I push myself to keep going and only consider getting out once the clock reads 47:00. I continue swimming laps upon laps. I don't count them, I don't keep track. I just swim. Finally, the clock tells me that I can get out without feeling guilty, and I approach the ladder. Once in the locker room I shower, dress and pack my swim bag back up. I am unsure if I will return to the evening session considering that it is in the middle of dinner time. But I make a promise to myself to attend the morning and afternoon session on Wednesday. I have to. Swimming is saving me.

I attend therapy bi-weekly. I take medications and get adequate sleep. But I also swim. Swimming gives me something to look forward to. Something to get out of bed for. Something to commit to and something to use my energy on when I have a lot of it. Swimming is also forgiving when I am too depressed to go, unlike school or work. As my tan darkens, and slowly my body becomes more in shape, it also makes me feel good about myself. Swimming is another piece of my wellness pie and it is just as important as all the other pieces.

Chapter 6
Growing up

What I heard when I was growing up:

You are such a worry-wart.
Stop crying, you're going to make yourself sick.
Enough with the pity party.
Just stop.
If you would just get out there, you would feel better.
It's hormones.

Stop making a mountain out of a molehill.
Suck it up.
Stop being dramatic.
You're being a damn baby.
You're just lazy.
It's all in your head.
You do this to yourself, you know.
You're fine, quit it.
Get over it.
Enough already!
You're doing this for attention.
Are you doing this to fit in?
You're wasting your life.

What I hear from my 30-year-old brain every.single.day:
Stop being so dramatic.
Just stop.
You're making this all up for attention.
Get over it.
Stop acting like this.
What a waste of a life.
What a baby you are.
You're immature.
This is all for attention.
You're making this all up.
What a fucking baby.

The time period in which I grew up, it was simply not thought of for a child to have a mental illness. Mental illness itself was a taboo subject so for a child to have it? Impossible. Growing up, my symptoms were ridiculed, not validated, mistaken for attention seeking behavior and mistaken for personality flaws. Relatives, teachers, friends and even psychologists that I saw did not see my quirks as symptoms of a mental illness. Instead, they saw it as something that needed to be worked on, by me. I was to blame for this. I was to blame for my actions and responses. It was me who had to fix this. "Tough love" was given often. I was pushed into situations which only increased my anxiety. I was ripped out of the bed when depressed. I was called "painfully shy" when instead it was Generalized Anxiety Disorder which is partly Social Anxiety. My symptoms were not taken seriously. When I would openly weep, I was told I was going to make myself sick. So I began to hide in my bedroom and cry. When I became obsessed with a topic or activity while hypomanic, I was congratulated on finally finding a hobby that I liked. Three or four days later when I would come down and abandon the project or hobby, I was ridiculed for losing interest, again, like i had so many other times before.

The symptoms of my mental illness were not understood by those around me. Of course, I do not blame them. Their ignorance to the symptoms of a mental illness was simply due to the time period. Bipolar II wasn't even officially recognized until recently and even then, psychologists were reluctant to diagnose it, let alone diagnose a child with it. My friends, family and others were not trying to be cruel and hateful, but rather they did not understand. They simply did not know. Unfortunately, there are still relatives of mine who do not understand and accept that I have a mental illness even though I have told them in detail my diagnosis and they have seen my symptoms with their own eyes.

Even though my relatives did not understand, damage was done. The examples I gave at the beginning of this chapter are true. And now, at 30 years old, I find myself telling myself these same things. I also find it difficult to accept my diagnosis or even accept that I have a mental illness all together. At times, I feel that what I have is a bad personality. I compare myself to my peers who have buckets without holes, who have established careers and college degrees. I hate myself for not being as successful as them because I convince myself that I am the same as them, even though I am not. I have a mental illness that has caused me to struggle in life and I forget that it is because of that, that I struggle, not because of a flawed personality or a choice I have made.

Sometimes, I even believe that I am making it all up for attention. That this is all a big act out of boredom. Unfortunately, I have been accused of this by relatives. But it begs the question, how have I maintained this act? I began having symptoms at the age of 4. Did I play out panic attacks for attention when I myself didn't even know what a panic attack was? How did I make up symptoms to mimic bipolar disorder when I didn't even know Bipolar II existed? For more than twenty years, symptom after symptom, I have maintained this straightforward disorder? And if it is out of boredom, wouldn't I find something else to do besides be depressed, which has nearly ruined my life? I find myself asking myself these same questions when I begin to believe that I am making it all up for attention and the evidence glares at me. This is not an act. It is not a made up disorder. I do have a mental illness and I always have.

Chapter 7
Questioning my Diagnosis

I frequent a forum for Bipolar Disorder. I usually read the entries daily and rarely respond. I find comfort reading that others are struggling like I am. So I read their struggles knowing that I can relate to how they feel. It is comforting, after feeling so alone for so long, to find others that are just like me.

One topic is brought up time and time again. Over and over. In my own mind, but also in the minds of others.

"What if I am not Bipolar? What if I am making this all up for attention? What if I really am in control of my moods and behaviors but I just choose not to be? What if everyone else actually DOES deal with what I deal with, but I am just overly emotional/sensitive? What if this is all just a figment of my imagination? What if this is all made up? What if I am not Bipolar but instead I am just a loser? What if my diagnosis is wrong, and there is nothing wrong with me except my inability to deal with everyday life issues?"

Searching "Am I really bipolar?" or "Questioning my diagnosis" in any bipolar forum will bring up pages upon pages of people who also go through this thought process. It is frequent.

I want to stop taking my medication. Cancel all therapy appointments. Stop going to the doctor. Get a job and continue with my life. What the fuck am I doing, taking this vacation of agonizing loneliness? Get a JOB! Suck it up buttercup. Pull up your big girl panties and march on. Carry on my wayward son.

Is there really anything actually genuinely wrong with me? Am I just playing a game?

But then I list out all of my outbursts. All of my breakdowns. My familiar waves, the fog of depression, my OH-MY-GOD ideas and pursuits which are never followed through to fruition. My embarrassing delusions of having romantic relationships with coworkers, professors, bosses and friends. The panic attacks and getting out of bed means climbing a mountain. Then I realize that that list is long. It is several pages long. An old company listed on my employee file that I was "mentally unstable", a label I scoffed at then, but now realize was a correct description.

But is that all real? Do I really have a problem or am I just weak?

This is why it is hard to stay on track with medication. This is why it is hard to continue to go to therapy every week. This is why it took me until the age of 30 to seek help.

Chapter 8
Who am I?

When I realized I had Bipolar Disorder, a light bulb switched on. After all these years, everything made sense. My quirks and approach to life had a medical reason. All those times I would devote my life to a project or cause, to then walk away a few days later with no emotion, had a medical cause. All of my questions about myself were answered. I finally knew why I had panic attacks, why social situations made my heart hyperventilate, why I had struggled with waves of depression since the 6th grade. My dozens of issues all fit nicely and neatly in a bag titled "Bipolar Disorder Type II". The comorbidity of an anxiety disorder with Bipolar is extremely high (over 85%) so all of my anxieties were explained as well. Everything made sense.

But it left me with one question: Where does Bipolar end, and I begin? If my quirks are bipolar. If my habits and overall demeanor, my sensitive nature, overly emotional reactions and my anxious personality are all attributed to a mental health disorder, then who is genuinely Sarah?

If I list out all of my most prominent personality traits in bullet points, and then cross off each bullet point that is a bipolar symptom, I would have essentially nothing left to attribute to my own personality.

Furthermore, and most troubling, is my ability and desire to write. I began writing when I was in junior high. I have always kept journals, written poetry and written short stories. For a time, I wrote for a newspaper, I have written and composed countless newsletters and short magazines and here I am writing again. There is a very strong link between creativity/intelligence and mental illnesses, particularly, Bipolar Disorder.

So, my most valued trait, my ability and love of writing, is present only because I have Bipolar Disorder? The very thing that has allowed me to pass school, express my severe emotions, and has paved my path in life, is essentially a symptom of a mental illness I posses?

Where do I begin? What is not attributed to Bipolar? Some would argue that my having Bipolar is simply who I am, and there is no need or purpose to attempt to separate myself from it. It simply is, and I simply am. But even then, I wonder who I would be, and what I would do, if I did not have Bipolar?

My quirks and eccentricities, writing, sensitive nature, anxious demeanor and overall personality is a result of having Bipolar II. Bipolar is who I am. I have read many articles demanding that "Bipolar does not define me" and "I am not Bipolar, I HAVE Bipolar" but I personally disagree. My Bipolar is who I am. It is my personality. It is my goals. It is my fears. It is my anxieties. It is my nightmares. It is me. Where do I begin? I begin with Bipolar.

Chapter 9
I am 30 years old

I am 30 years old. I don't know what I am doing. I take 5 different medications a day and I have been admitted to a psych ward twice, and three times I have stayed only overnight. I don't know if I should continue my therapy and medication, or if I should just throw it all away and "continue with my life" like I tell myself to do all the time. It's as if I am choosing to be this way. Others see me as choosing to be this way, so why can't I? It certainly feels like a lifestyle choice. I'm 30 years old and I feel that my life has been a waste. My time has been thrown away. My opportunities ignored. I am 30 years old and I have tried to attend college six times, but each time my depression ruins it and I drop out, again. I am 30 years old and I have never held a professional job that thinks highly of me. Instead they think I am emotionally unstable and in need of psychiatric help. I am 30 years old and I am struggling with an invisible illness. I experience emotions far beyond the usual scope of normality. I struggle to function sometimes. And other times I function way better than I should. I am extremely productive, confident, happy and full of ideas.

I am 30 years old and the medication is working. My depression was almost chronic except for the occasional hypomania. The depression would last for months, and then I would have a hypomanic break to return to depression again. But the medication is working now. My depression lasts for days, not weeks. Hypomania is almost non-existent (which I mourn a bit). For the first time in my life, I am not chronically suicidal. I have weeks of normality which I have never had before but always craved. Weeks where I am not overly emotional on the verge of tears at any given moment. But instead I am stable.

Being stable can be frustrating all on it's own as well. I feel confident that I could hold a job or return to school and I even put in applications or start applying for classes. But then I have a wave of "breakthrough depression" that immobilizes me. To my blanket burrito I go, back to feeling like a parasite, a waste of space, a waste of life. While I am "stable", I will never be normal-stable, only my version of stable. I will probably always have depression. I will probably always have hypomania. I will probably always have anxiety. But with therapy, medication, swimming and routine, I will have my own version of "stable" that will allow me to live a somewhat normal life.

When I was first diagnosed, I had a moment of clarity. I was delusional that there were cameras installed in the ceiling of our house and I was being watched. In that moment, I realized how sick I was. I realized that I did, in fact, have a mental illness and it was taking over my life. I began to sob profusely because I realized how sick I was but also that this is chronic, lifelong. Every day, every week, every year, for the rest of my life I will deal with this disorder in one way or another. This is not something that will delightfully go away when I feel like it's a good time. There will never be a time that I am completely symptom free. There is a small percentage of that happening, but because of the severity of my Bipolar and the length of time that I have had it, untreated, being symptom free is not going to happen for me. I will also have to take pills for the rest of my life, and they will always be neatly organized in a pill container to avoid fumbling with numerous bottles a day.

I am 30 years old and I have Bipolar Disorder Type II and Generalized Anxiety Disorder. I am also a wife, a mother, a writer, a photographer and a swimmer. I am doing the very best I can.

Chapter 10
Bipolar Disorder Type II

After being diagnosed, I found very little information about Bipolar Type II. Most of the articles I read were centered around Type I, thus, Mania. When I went to the library, I found only 3 books on Bipolar. Each book only had a page or two on Bipolar II, the rest of the book was about Bipolar I and Mania. I became very frustrated to not have readable material on my diagnosis because while Type I & II are both technically "Bipolar", they are very different in nature. For this reason, I have decided to write the article that I wish that I had come across when I was first diagnosed. Below, you will find a well researched article which contains facts pertaining to Type II which are pulled from medical journals and other credible sources.

In 1994, Bipolar Type II was officially added to the DSM-IV, which is the Diagnostic Manual used by Psychiatrists and Therapists to diagnose individuals. For the first time, it became officially recognized that individuals had a variation of Bipolar disorder. Some refer to it as a "milder" form of the disorder but this is woefully incorrect. Severe depression is more prevalent in Type II, and frequent mood changes is also more common in Type II. Furthermore, Type II has a higher suicide rate than any other mental illness and drug abuse is more common than Type I. (Frances, A. & Jones, K. D. (2012). Bipolar disorder type II revisited. *Bipolar Disorders,* 14, 474-477.) Some argue that Type II is more chronic considering that patients typically rapidly cycle, are more symptomatic and treatment is often more complicated. While Type I patients may experience depression only once, Type II's typically live in a nearly constant state of depression only breaking for hypomanic episodes. The Mania in Type I is the most obvious difference as Type II's do not experience manic episodes but instead experience hypomania. The Symptoms for hypomania are inflated self esteem, decreased need for sleep, intensified and pressured speech, racing thoughts, easily distracted by minor details, goal directed activities (i.e. projects, obsessively writing), psychomotor agitation (i.e. pacing) and excessive involvement in pleasurable activities that have risky consequences. (*http://www.jbrf.org/diagnosis-by-the-dsm/*) While a manic episode is more extreme in nature and often involves losing touch with reality, a hypomanic episode can be as simple as energetically painting your house at 3 a.m. or spending four days writing music. Of course, in order to be qualified as a hypomanic episode, it must last for at least four days, however it is not uncommon to have shorter hypomanic episodes as well.

Depression is the ugly monster of Type II Bipolar Disorder. Depression is severe, frequent and typically becomes more severe if left untreated. The symptoms of depression are the same for regular depression (loss of interest in pleasurable activities, low or down mood, low self esteem, etc.) however, Type II often involves atypical depression. "Atypical depression is a subtype of major depression or dysthymic disorder that involves several specific symptoms, including increased appetite or weight gain, sleepiness or excessive sleep, marked fatigue or weakness, moods that are strongly reactive to environmental circumstances, and feeling extremely sensitive to rejection."

(*http://www.webmd.com/depression/guide/atypical-depression*)

Bipolar II patients have a more chronic course, significantly more depressive episodes, and shorter periods of being well between episodes than patients with type I. Bipolar II disorder is highly associated with the risk for suicide. (*New York Times,* "Bipolar Disorder")

Hypomanic episodes are often under the radar. They can be seen as a depressive person simply having a really good few days. Hypomanic episodes can be as simple as rearranging furniture for hours on end, exercising more than usual, manically writing songs or a book or becoming obsessed with a new hobby or interest. The hallmark trait of hypomania is the lack of sleep and the feeling of not needing sleep. Staying up until 3 or 4 in the morning writing music to then take a small nap and wake up feeling refreshed, or not sleeping at all. Hypomania feels like you have drank several pots of coffee. Your self esteem is very high, you feel very sexual, social, funny and intelligent.

Because most people only seek mental health treatment in depressive episodes, Bipolar II is usually misdiagnosed as Major Depressive Disorder at first because who would seek mental health help when they are on a hypomanic high? The typically atypical symptoms of depression leaves the person feeling heavy, weak, achy and sensitive to intersocial rejection, that is, when others reject you or show they dislike you. Depression is easy to diagnose and Bipolar II is easily misdiagnosed as unipolar depression. Typically, only after the patient is properly assessed is a Bipolar II diagnosis given.

Bipolar II patients typically rotate between hypomania and depression that lasts for weeks or months. This constant rotation of moods can feel like you are in a washing machine on spin cycle. Once a proper diagnosis is given, a patient is then given proper medication which is not a simple antidepressant. Instead, they are given a mood stabilizer paired with an antidepressant, among other medications as needed for the patient.

Bipolar II is sometimes referred to as "hidden bipolar" because it is so easily mistaken for unipolar depression. When treated as unipolar depression, patients are not given the proper medication as they are given antidepressants which can cause a full blown manic episode or can cause the depression to be worse and longer than usual. Bipolar I effects 1% of the population while Type II effects 2%. Many people with Type II never seek treatment because they don't recognize the symptoms of bipolar II. Some with Bipolar II are so high functioning that they don't even need treatment and are quite successful in the professional world.